JIAMOND

AN AFRICAN AMERICAN BALLERINA

Bernetta Watson; Jiamond

AuthorHouse™
1663 Liberty Drive
Bloomington, IN 47403
www.authorhouse.com
Phone: 833-262-8899

This book is printed on acid-free paper.

ISBN: 978-1-6655-2316-5 (sc)
ISBN: 978-1-6655-2317-2 (e)

Print information available on the last page.

Published by AuthorHouse 04/19/2021

authorHOUSE®

DIAMOND

"Follow your dreams"

Jiamond

Author, Bernetta "Breezy" Watson

Jiamond an African American Ballerina

Jiamond age 5 years old

Contents

Included in this book are the meaning of some words used in this book.

Dedication

This book is dedicated to Jiamond's late Grandmother. Rev. Cora Elizabeth Moore, February 3, 1926-June 30, 2019. Cora always believed in Jiamond's dance ability.

Jiamond danced in the D.C. CAP. Stars 2015 competition at the Kennedy Center Washington D.C. Jiamond won a $10,000 Scholarship award. Cora remarks to me "I knew she would win"

Preface

HOW BALLERINA OF COLOR ARE CHANGING THE PALETTE OF DANCE.

Black and brown dancers are using their minds, bodies and conviction to change the world of ballet, inside and out.

2017 Daphne M. Lee Miss Black USA, is a ballerina. She has done research on the role of black hair styles in ballet.

2019 Charlotte Nebres 11 years old became the first black to be given the role of Marie in the Christmas play the NutCracker in the New York City Ballet Production.

HuffPost 2020 by Rohina Katoch Sehra
Black History Month 2020

"Girls follow your dreams"   Jiamond

Introduction

The journey of becoming a professional dancer is long and hard. You must be passionate and have confidence in yourself. Never forget your love for dance and the power in dance and your training, remember to keep your head up and have fun. What doesn't kill you makes you stronger.!!!!!

"Dreams are like stars, there are a million in the sky but we only see a few. Let your light shine bright and your dreams will come true".

Jiamond is telling all young girls to "follow your dreams."

Jiamond is a beautiful young lady. She has a very warm smile. She is self-motivated, respectful to others, has positive self-esteem, positive self-confidence. She is well-mannered and uses proper etiquette.

When dancing in a show she is very professional. She is always aware of her personal appearance, personal hygiene. Her hair is always well groomed. Her make-up for her shows is always professional.

Jiamond has goals and dreams. She will graduate from the University of the Arts with a Bachelors of Fine Arts degree in May, 2020.

Biography

Jiamond was born February 22, 1998, in Fort Washington Maryland, she lived with her parents and three brothers.

Education: elementary and middle school she attended the John Hanson French Immersion School located in Oxon Hill, Maryland.

High school: Duke Ellington School of the Arts, located in Washington, D.C.

College: University of the Arts, class of 2020, located in Philadelphia, Pa.

Jiamond first dance school was Expression Dance Theater, located in Oxon Hill, Maryland.

BodyMoves DanceWork, located in Fort Washington, Maryland.

Jiamond's parents told me that she has been dancing since she was 1 year old. Her mother Tia taught dance in her home.

John, Jiamond's father built a dance studio for Tia to teach her students dance. Jiamond would find her way into the dance studio, she was a toddler so she would crawl around on the floor often getting in the way of students.

What I remember about Jiamond as a toddler, when she would hear music, she always would dance, even if it was a car radio she would dance on the sidewalk. She would dance all over the house always jumping on and off furniture.

Jiamond at age 3 years of would teach her neighborhood playmates how to dance.

Jiamond realized at age 6 years old that she wanted to be a professional dancer.

Jiamond love to read. She speaks French, enjoy going to the movies. Her favorite foods are steamed crabs and macaroni and cheese. Jiamond would really enjoy her holiday and summer visits to Nana house in Hampton, Virginia, because they always had a seafood feast that included steamed crabs, fried fish and cornbread.

Jiamond has a sewing machine, she likes to sew when she has the time.

Her favorite colors are blue, green and red.

Jiamond loves animals, she has a dog named Ali, he lives with family friends because of school she was unable to care for him, she does visit him and still love him.

Jiamond did volunteer one summer, while in middle school at an animal hospital in Waldorf Maryland.

Jiamond did talk about being a veterinarian and a dancer.

Jiamond also enjoy travel, her favorite place to travel is Virginia Beach, Virginia. She enjoys the summer sun, warm sand and the beach water. Her travel in Virginia has been to the following cities, Hampton, Newport News, Williamsburg, Jamestown, Norfolk, Phoebus and Doswell, these visits have been on family vacations. Jiamond did visit Puerto Rico last year with her family. Jiamond dance career has afforded her the opportunity to travel for training and auditions. Her travel included Los Angeles, San Francisco, Dallas, Texas, Cleveland, Ohio. New York City, Harlem New York, Atlanta Georgia, and Philadelphia Pa.

Jiamond wants to let all young dancers know, it is not easy, you must work hard. Jiamond told me that she knew that she had to be in good physical condition, exercise and practice daily and keep her mind focused, get proper rest, relaxation, proper nutrition and water intake.

Jiamond wants all dancers to know you will need good social skills, communication skills, personal hygiene and personal appearance are very important. You must know how to make make a good first impression.

It is important to be aware of your body language and attitude.

Talent is not always enough. A dancer must be able to work with people, choreographers want to work with nice people.

Jiamond gives her high school credit in helping her to prepare for her dance career. Jiamond was a 2016 graduate of Duke Ellington School of the Arts, located in Washington D.C.

She also attended Life Skills, Etiquette and Leadership Workshops. Learning about good manners proper etiquette and life skills.

Social Skills

Social skills we use them to communicate and interact with each other both verbally and non-verbally through gestures, body language and our personal appearance.

Social skills and interpersonal skills are important to relate to one another.

Jiamond learned that you must have good communication skills, good listening skills, good manners and proper etiquette.

Making a good first impression is very important. You only get one chance to make a good first impression. It takes less than 30 seconds to make an impression. When people make their decision of their impression of you, it is based on your actions, energy and the way you present yourself.

Personal Hygiene is very important. It will help you have positive self-esteem and positive self-confidence.

Bathing and using deodorant is important.

Change underwear daily.

Brush your teeth on a regular basis. Always in the morning and at bedtime.

Good personal hygiene can help improve your self-confidence and maintain good health.

Health awareness always wash your hands to prevent spreading germs. Wash your hand for 20 seconds. Sing the birthday song it is 20 seconds. Wash your hands before each meal, after playing outdoors, after playing with your pet, after playing games after using bathroom and often as you feel you need to.

No chipped nail polish.

Personal appearance is equally as important

Always be well groomed, hair neat, skin clean, make up age appropriate. Small size earrings. Clothes need to be pressed, clean and fitting properly, not to tight or to short.

Shoes, stocking or socks clean, neat coordinating with your outfit.

Good Manners

Manners is polite social behavior.

What are some good manners to know and use?

1. Greet everyone with a warm smile and a hello. Always speak when you walk into a room.

2. Say "Please" and May I ask before you take something from someone else.

3. Asking May I: Always say Please.

4. Say Thank you when someone gives you something.

5. Never interrupt elders when they are talking, say "excuse me, please."

6. Respect other's opinions never try to impose your opinion on someone.

7. Respect everyone's opinion. Every individual is different and unique.

8. Knock on a door before entering and waits to be told to come in.

9. Sticking a tongue out could indicate that a person is being rude.

Teasing

Playful

Taunting

Mocking

It is not good manners for a child to stick their tongue out at an adult.

It is a form of body language that is not acceptable in our society and culture.

Some good tips on Table Manners

1. Elbow off table

2. Sit up in your chair

3. Chew with your mouth closed

4. Do not talk with food in your mouth. You can choke on food if you are talking and swallowing at the same time. No one wants to see the food in your mouth.

5. Take small sip of your liquid from your glass or cup.

6. Use your napkin

7. Don't talk about things at the table that will gross others out. "Dead animals" "vomit, using the bathroom" "bleeding from a cut or wound."

8. Do not reach across the table ask someone to pass the food item that you need.

9. Always pass the salt and pepper at the same time.

Proper Etiquette

Meaning of Etiquette is a code of polite behavior and following rules in our society.

Some example of following etiquette rules.

1. Be yourself

2. Say "Thank You"

3. Give genuine compliment and accept compliments that are given to you with a Thank You.

4. Don't be boastful, arrogant or loud.

5. Do not criticize or complain

6. Be on time

7. Do not wear your pajamas in a public place.

These Are Jiamond's Favorite Dance Types

Horton technique

Hip hop

African dance

Tap dance

Jazz dance

Contemporary dance styles

Ballet

Positive Advice from Jiamond to Dancers

1. Set goals, make a vision board. Get your mom, sister or grandmother to help you.

2. Follow your dreams

3. Be a leader

4. Get good grades in school, focus on your education.

5. Be strong

6. Honest

7. Truthful

8. Be Persistent

9. Be all you can be.

10. Always be kind to everyone

11. Love yourself

12. Be dedicated to your dreams.

Jiamond Has Goals And Dreams

Jiamond has a zeal for dance.

She will graduate from the University of the Arts with a Bachelors of Fine Arts Degree in May 2020.

Jiamond dreams to continue her career in dance. She would like to work for choreographers across the globe. However, Jiamond's dream job is dancer with Alonzo King LINES Ballet.

Jiamond would also like to pursue a career in sculptural design and creative non-fiction. She dreams of being a multi-media artists.

Jiamond's credits and accomplishments

1. A fellow dance artist with Ballet X, located Philadelphia, Pa. 2019-2020.

2. Presidents fund grant recipient

3. University of the Arts - Directors Scholarship recipient

4. $10,000 Scholarship recipient of DC Capital Stars.

5. Alonzo King Lines Ballet Summer Intensive (full scholarship)

   International Association of Blacks in Dance IABD touring conference for dancers

6. Alvin Ailey American Dance Theater (partial scholarship)

7. Dallas Black Dance Theater (full scholarship)

8. Debbie Allen Dance Academy

9. Shirley Chisholm Leadership Award from the National Congress of Black Women

New words that are in the book.

Giving you the meaning of the words. These words are educational and informative. The words will give you a better understanding and a delightful experience.

New Words

A WORDS

Ability- the power to do something well, skills or talent.

Accomplishment- something that has been achieved successfully.

Achieve- complete a task with a successful end.

Appearance- things that are visually seen when you look at a person.

B WORDS

Ballerina- A female dancer in a ballet company.

Ballet- an artistic form of dance.

BalletX- a dance company, located in Philadelphia Pa.

Behavior- the kind of action a person does (good or bad)

Biography- an account of a person's life written by someone else.

Body language- communication nonverbally through conscious or unconscious gesture and movement of the body. People can read your body language and make a decision of how they think you feel about what is being said to you.

C WORDS

Choreograph- plan how a dancer will move.

Communication Skills is a way information is exchanged between individuals through common symbols and signs or behavior.

Competition- the act of trying to do better than others especially to win a game or contest.

Confidence- a feeling of faith in yourself.

D WORDS

Dance- to move with rhythmic steps motions in time to music.

Dedicated- something written that says who a book or work of art was created for.

Dedication- to commit yourself fully to something.

Dream- a story or a picture that happens in your mind when you sleep.

E WORDS

Etiquette- a set of rules that tell people how to behave in social situations.

Etiquette has to do with good manners. It is not so much our own manners but making other people feel comfortable by the way we treat them.

F WORDS

Favorite- what you like the most.

Fellow- ballet dancer that is in training with a ballet company, apprentice

Focus- concentrate attention or energy on something.

Fortitude- strength of mind allows one to deal with adversity with courage.

G WORDS

Goals- something that you hope to achieve in the future.

Good- means doing things well. A good thing when people like it.

Good- can also mean that something helps you to be healthy.

H WORDS

Hygiene- practice such as washing your hands or keeping your body clean to prevent disease.

I WORDS

Impeccable- the highest standard in appearance.

Impression- an opinion or idea about someone formed with taught.

Instructor- person who teaches or tells you how to do something.

J WORDS

Jazz- is an African music that began in New Orleans, Louisiana in 1917.

K WORD

Kind- to be kind is to try to help others. To be helpful, considerate and gentle.

L WORD

Learn- is being taught.

Listening- is a great way to communicate. Listening is to hear with thoughtful attention and consideration.

M WORD

Manners- polite social behavior.
Having respect for others being kind and treating people like you want to treated.

N WORD

Nice- pleasant, agreeable, satisfactory and kind.

O WORD

Obey- follow a request or direction given by another person.
Example: I always obey my dance instructor.

Optimistic- hopeful and confident about the future.

P WORDS

Persistent to continue in a course of action in spite of difficulty or opposition.

Positive- to be a positive person you most be confident, optimistic and believe in yourself.

Q WORDS

Quiet- making little or no noise: "Be quiet and listen"

R WORDS

Respect- feeling of deep admiration or like for someone or something because of their abilities and achievements.

Rude- impolite or ill-mannered not nice or kind words.

Example: That's a rude thing to say. "Your dress is not pretty."
Why are you so rude to your friends?
"Go home" I am not playing with you.

S WORDS

SOCIAL SKILLS is knowing how to get along with other people. You should begin to learn social skills as a toddler, when you are being told by your mother and teacher to share your toys to play nice with other children. Learning how to interact with others and respecting others space. Knowing how to say please and thank you, excuse me, may I have some cookies, speaking kindly to your friends.

T WORDS

Teach- to teach is to give information so that someone can learn or understand something by experience.

Technique-skill in performing the basic operation of an art.

U WORD

Underwear- clothes worn under your top clothes like your bra, panties. You always will need to change into clean underwear after each bath or shower because these items can cause body odor, also make sure you use deodorant to prevent underarm odor.

V WORDS

Veterinarian- is a doctor who takes care of animals.

Vacation- a time of rest from work, school or other regular activities.

Vision- ability to look ahead in the imagination.

Vision Board- is a collage of images, pictures and affirmations of one desires, designed to serve as a source of inspiration and motivation and to use the law of attraction to attain goals.

W WORD

Work is the energy you use to do or make something. It is also a means of making a form of income.

X WORD

None listed

Y WORD

Young- being early stage of life or growth.

Z WORD

Zeal- great energy or enthusiasm in pursuit of a cause or an object.

Hope the meaning of these words have been helpful, educational, informative and a learning experience.

Thank you!

Bernetta Watson

Bernetta "Breezy" Watson received her certification from the international school of Protocol located in Hunt Valley Maryland in 2005. She is the author of 3 etiquette books for pre-teen and teens.

Bernetta is the founder and director of Manners Unlimited Etiquette and Leadership Workshop located in Hampton Virginia. She is the director and founder of the Miss Social Etiquette/image Pageant.

She conducts workshops in social skills, civility skills, communications kills and table manners.

She realizes that in our hurried life style the need to teach this skill is very much needed.

Jiamond

Co-author

Printed in the United States
by Baker & Taylor Publisher Services